It's Heartly Fare

A food book that makes sense
of fat, cholesterol and salt

By: Timothy S. Harlan, MD

This book was written to help you better understand what you are being told about fat, cholesterol and salt. It is not to replace your health care provider's advice. Also, it is not a guide for children under 2, and pregnant women should not use this book without their doctor's OK.

Welcome

You've got this book in your hands because you need to change your diet in some way. (Or maybe you picked it up to swat a bug!) Whatever the reason, if you're thinking about a new way of eating, you most likely have a lot of questions about food.

The main goal of your new way of eating is to cut down on fat, cholesterol and salt. Make this the one rule that you return to over and over as you learn. Repeat this goal as you walk down the aisle of the grocery store:

Cut down on fat, cholesterol and salt.
Cut down on fat, cholesterol and salt.
Cut down on fat, cholesterol and salt.

When you finish **It's Heartly Fare,** you will speak a new language and know how to eat for better health.

> ***The best thing about this book:***
> *If you do nothing more than eat what is suggested here, you will be on your way to eating a healthy heart diet. So dig in.*
>
> *We have tried to make this book easy to read and understand. We have also prepared a practice supplement to help you plan a diet, shop for healthy foods and eat out.*

Table of contents

- Getting started 4-11
  - Fats 6-7
  - Cholesterol 8-9
  - Sodium (salt) 10-11
- Some really good guys 12
- Some really bad guys 13
- Fat days 14
- Read all labels 15-26
- Things you might not know about some foods 27-35
- Eating out 36-39
- Cooking it yourself 40-46
- More food talk 47-55
- Bye 56

Introduction 3

Getting Started
MENU

Most doctors and registered dietitians (RDs) suggest this type of healthy eating plan:

✓ **Eat very little fat and cholesterol.**
This means less fatty meats, organ meats, egg yolks, whole milk dairy foods and fried foods. It also means less high-fat sweets like ice cream, cakes, pies and chocolate.

✓ **Eat less salt (sodium).**
This most often means no more than 1 teaspoon or about 2,000 mg per day, unless your doctor says to eat less. Many foods have sodium in them, so you need to limit salt added during cooking as well as at the table.

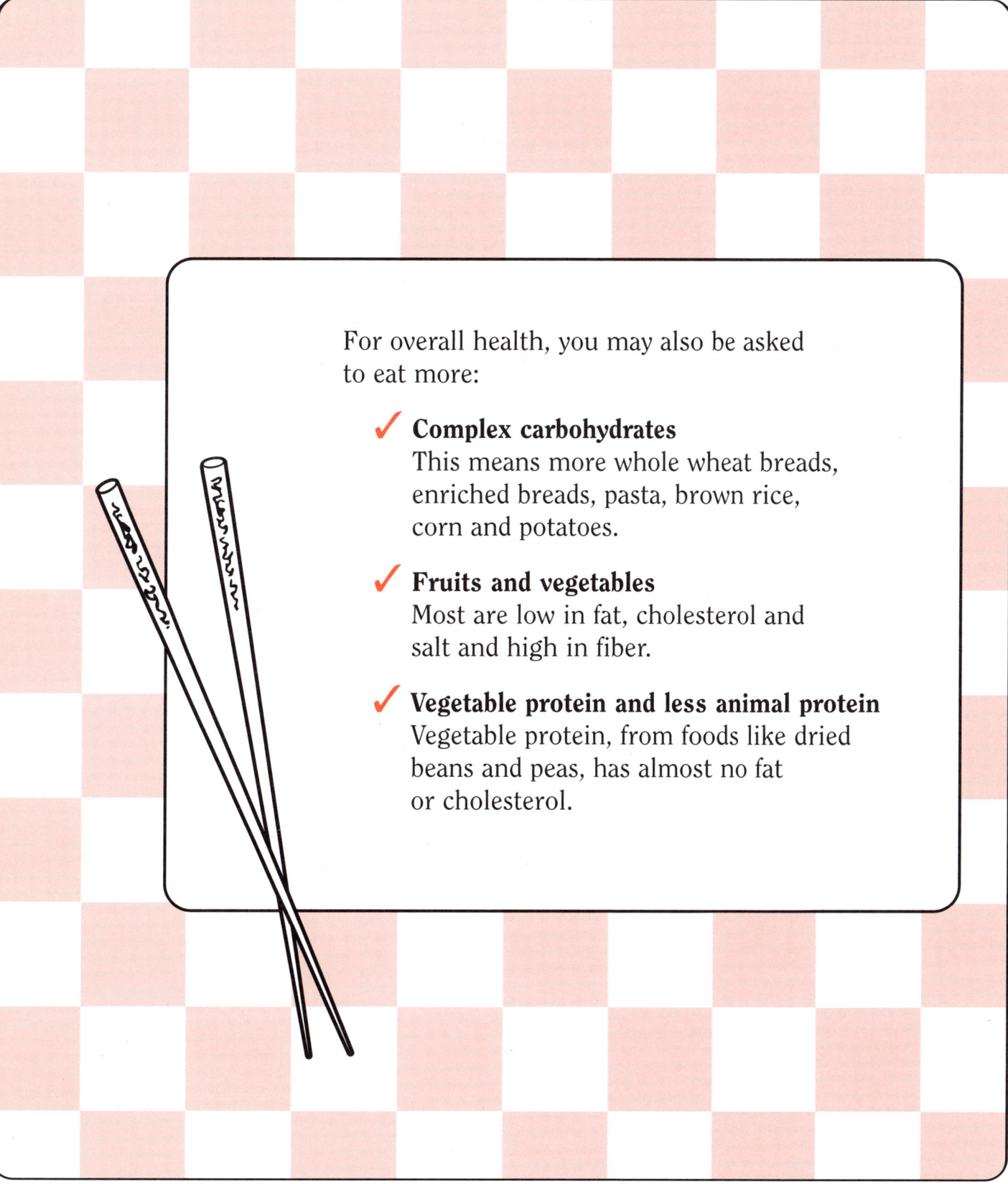

For overall health, you may also be asked to eat more:

✓ **Complex carbohydrates**
This means more whole wheat breads, enriched breads, pasta, brown rice, corn and potatoes.

✓ **Fruits and vegetables**
Most are low in fat, cholesterol and salt and high in fiber.

✓ **Vegetable protein and less animal protein**
Vegetable protein, from foods like dried beans and peas, has almost no fat or cholesterol.

What you are up against:

Fats

Diets high in **saturated fats** have been linked to heart disease. Saturated fats raise the cholesterol level in the blood. This is the kind of fat that you don't want to eat too much of.

You find saturated fats in animal foods like steak, butter and cheese. Animal foods like these also have cholesterol in them. Vegetable foods don't have cholesterol, but many do have saturated fats—foods like solid margarines, coconut and palm oils, nuts and chocolate.

Eating too much fat (especially saturated fat) can be bad for you. This is even more true if your blood cholesterol level is high.

Look at these food choices. By choosing one food over another, you can control how much fat you eat.

HIGH IN FAT	A BETTER CHOICE
1 cup of whole milk (8g fat)	1 cup of skim milk (less than ½g fat)
1 plain chocolate bar (9g fat)	½ cup fat-free chocolate pudding or 1 fat-free Fudgesickle (0g fat)
1 cheeseburger (14g fat)	1 plain burger (10g fat)
½ cup Häagen Dazs ice cream (16g fat)	½ cup nonfat frozen yogurt (0g fat)

The grams (g) of fat are listed on a food label. A *gram* is a unit or way of measuring contents of foods. Fats, proteins and carbohydrates are measured in grams. Cholesterol and sodium are measured in milligrams (mg). There are 1,000 mg in a gram.

Unsaturated fats are OK for you in small amounts. There are 2 kinds of these fats:

- *mono*unsaturated **(canola, olive** and **peanut oils)**
- *poly*unsaturated **(safflower, sunflower, corn, cottonseed, soybean** and **sesame oils)**

What you have to keep in mind about oils is that **all are high in fat and calories, even if they are the right kinds to eat.** One tablespoon of any oil has 14g of fat and 120 calories in it. **Use only a little.**

Getting started

Cholesterol

Heart attacks and strokes have been linked to high cholesterol levels in the blood.

Pure cholesterol, a sort of waxy, yellow junk, is in every cell in the body. Your body makes some cholesterol, and it's also found in animal foods. Cholesterol is used to make hormones, digest food and build cells. But you only need a small amount. If you eat more cholesterol (**and** saturated fat) than your body can use or get rid of, the excess hangs around gummin' up the arteries.

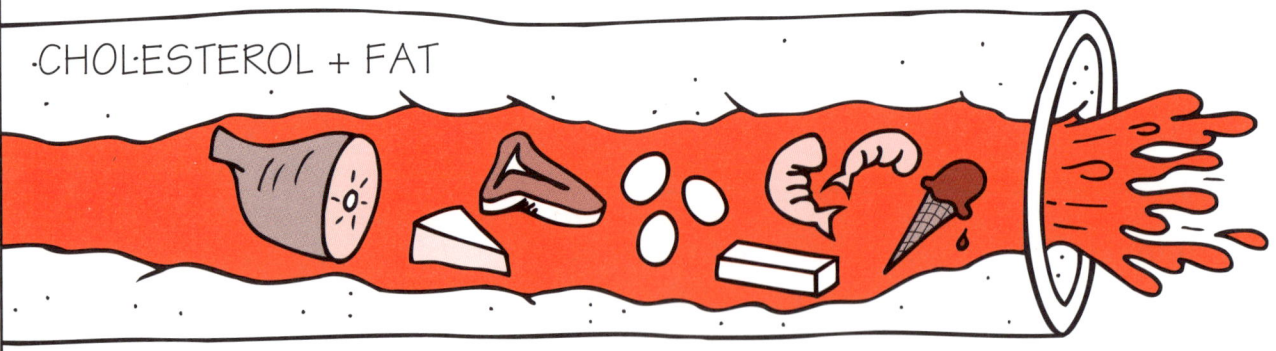

CHOLESTEROL + FAT

BLOOD VESSEL

Most likely your doctor will want you to eat less than 300mg of cholesterol per day. You can see by these foods how fast cholesterol adds up.

HIGH IN CHOLESTEROL	A BETTER CHOICE
1 Tbs butter (35mg cholesterol)	1 Tbs margarine (0mg cholesterol)
1 cup whole milk pudding (32mg cholesterol)	1 cup skim milk pudding (0mg cholesterol)
1 egg yolk (200-250mg cholesterol)	1 serving egg substitute (0mg cholesterol)
4 oz steamed shrimp (174mg cholesterol)	4 oz steamed scallops (60mg cholesterol)

The milligrams of cholesterol are listed on food labels. Some foods will brag "No Cholesterol," but be careful. The food may have no cholesterol, but it can have up to 2g of saturated fat per serving which can raise your blood cholesterol level.

These can help lower total blood cholesterol and also help raise the HDL* (good cholesterol):

- regular exercise
- losing weight
- not smoking

*See p. 51.

Sodium (salt to most of us!)

Salt is made from sodium and chloride.

Salt can make high blood pressure (hypertension) worse. The extra sodium can be a problem for people with high blood pressure, heart failure and kidney or prostate disease. Extra salt can also be a problem during pregnancy.

Many ready-to-eat foods you buy at the store and in restaurants have lots of salt in them. Most snack foods, lunch meats, pickles and fast foods are high in salt.

Check the **Nutrition Facts** on the package to see how much sodium a food has per serving.

From these food choices, you can see how easy it is to cut a lot of sodium from your diet.

HIGH IN SODIUM	A BETTER CHOICE
1 Louis Rich turkey hot dog (520mg sodium)	1 Hormel Light & Lean 97% fat-free hot dog (350mg sodium and less fat)
1 slice beef bologna (239mg sodium)	1 oz white chicken meat (65mg sodium)
1 cup canned vegetable soup (770mg sodium)	1 cup low-salt vegetable soup (67mg sodium)
1 Whopper with cheese (1164mg sodium)	1 plain Burger King burger with tomato and lettuce (509mg sodium)

Look for salt-free foods, and add the salt yourself. (Measure with care.) Or look for low-sodium foods. The milligrams of sodium are listed on food labels.

Seasonings like these have a lot of sodium:

- table salt or sea salt
- soy sauce (including "Lite")
- seasoned salts (including "Lite")
- baking powder
- baking soda
- onion salt, garlic salt, celery salt

You can find low-salt, salt-free or low-sodium versions of some of these in many grocery stores. (If you take medicine, ask your doctor if it's OK before you use these products.)

Getting started 11

Some really good guys

Here are some foods that are low in fat, cholesterol and/or salt. There are many more than we can list here. Add to this list as you find heart healthy foods.

- no-salt tomato foods
- Featherweight low-sodium baking powder
- Con Agra "Healthy Choice" & Weight Watcher's "Smart Ones" frozen meals
- Arnold Bakers "Light" oatmeal bread
- No Salt Added V8 or tomato juice
- Fleischmann's or Second Nature's egg beaters
- Polaner All Fruit Spreads
- low-fat, no-cholesterol mayo
- Prego No Salt Added spaghetti sauce
- tuna in spring water (no salt added)
- Kavli and Wasa Flatbread (crackers)
- fresh fish fillets
- lean meat fillets (flank steak, top round)
- light meat chicken or turkey (skinned)
- fresh scallops
- brown rice
- fresh fruits
- fresh or frozen (without salt) vegetables
- nonfat frozen yogurt
- nonfat or low-fat ice cream, ice milk
- angel food cake
- ginger snaps
- graham crackers
- Jell-O
- Dole Fruit and Juice Bars
- PAM olive or canola oil spray
- Mrs. Dash Steak Sauce
- Mrs. Dash herb mixtures
- nonfat sour cream, nonfat cream cheese
- nonfat cottage cheese

Some really bad guys

Here are some foods that are often high in either fat, cholesterol or salt. There are many more than we can list here. Add to this list as you find them.

- french fried onion rings
- french fries
- canned beans and hot dogs
- processed or cured hams
- hot dogs (turkey dogs are lower in fat than beef dogs, but they have a lot of sodium)
- potted meat
- vienna sausage
- bacon, sausage
- peanut butter
- packaged sauces, seasonings (such as chili, gravy, hollandaise)
- regular mayo
- creamed soups
- bouillon cubes (low-salt ones OK)
- bacon bits
- relishes, olives, pickles
- most cookies
- bakery cakes, pies, etc.
- potato chips, corn chips, cheese puffs, etc.
- refried beans (nonfat ones OK)
- frozen fried potatoes
- cheese (see p. 22)
- granola
- hamburger or tuna mixes
- worcestershire sauce
- soy or teriyaki sauce
- some non-dairy creamers (dry or liquid)

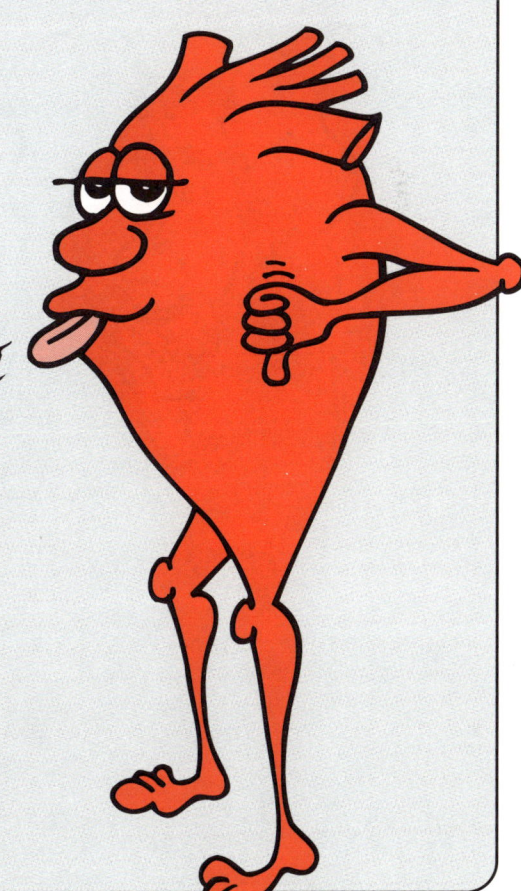

Fat days

There may be times when you eat more fat, cholesterol or salt than you want to. Special occasions, trips and dinners out are "slippery times" for careful eaters.

When "fat meals" happen, think about what you are eating for that whole day. If you ate too much of the wrong kinds of foods at one meal, eat very low-fat, low-cholesterol or low-salt foods for the rest of the day. Or if one day stacks up as a "fat day," eat very healthy foods for the next couple of days.

Your goal is to eat well as often as you can. It is not to be perfect. Don't panic when some fat, cholesterol or salt sneaks into your diet. Just get back to your healthy food choices at the next meal.

Read all labels

Finding the fat, cholesterol and salt in foods means **reading food labels.** It may seem like going on safari or a food hunt, but it can be fun. The next pages tell you what some of the words on a food label mean.

Reading books and pamphlets suggested by a registered dietitian or the American Dietetic Association can also help you learn about what's in the foods you like to eat.

Calorie-free or no calorie
Anything that says this must have less than 5 calories per serving.

No cholesterol, cholesterol-free
There is **less than 2mg of cholesterol** in the food. Foods labeled cholesterol-free must also have less than **2g of saturated fat per serving.** When a food claims to be "no cholesterol," it must also say if it is like all foods of its type. For example, a label might read, "Corn oil margarine, a no cholesterol food."

Nonfat or fat-free
The food has no more than ½g of fat per serving. The words **no-fat, no added fat** and **zero fat** mean the same thing as fat-free.

Unsalted or no sodium added
No salt has been added to the food.

Reduced calorie, fat, cholesterol or sodium
The food has at least 25% less fat, cholesterol, calories or sodium than the regular food. The words **less** or **fewer** mean the same as **reduced.**

Diet
Diet products must either be **low-calorie** or **reduced calorie** or have some other kind of special use in a diet.

Read all labels

Lite or light

This means the food has ⅓ fewer calories OR ½ the fat OR ½ the sodium of the regular food. Foods that are light in color or texture may also be labeled light. But the food company has to tell you when it uses light to refer to color or texture.

Healthy

A food labeled healthy must be a **low-fat and low-saturated fat food.** It must also have no more cholesterol or sodium than is recommended by the FDA. It does not mean the food is sugar-free.

There are some foods with the word "Healthy" in the brand name. If the brand name was used before 1989, the company is allowed to keep using the name. This may not mean that the food is as healthy as your diet needs to be. Check the label.

Natural

Watch out for this term. There is no guideline yet for what "natural" means. It could mean that the food has 50% lard or has a lot of sugar in it. "Natural" has nothing to do with whether or not a food is healthy.

Percent fat-free, % fat-free

Foods that claim to be a certain percent fat-free (like "97% fat-free") have to be **low-fat** foods. This means they must have 3g of fat or less per serving.

Read all labels

Low

When you see this with words like calorie or fat (as in low-fat or low-calorie) it means the same thing as the words **low source of, few, little** or **small amounts of.**

- **low-calorie** - 40 calories or less/serving
- **low-cholesterol** - 20mg or less chol./serving
- **low-fat** - 3g of fat or less/serving
- **low-saturated fat** - 1g or less saturated fat/serving
- **low-sodium** - 140mg or less sodium/serving
- **very low-sodium** - 35mg or less sodium/serving

Hydrogenated

Sometimes you will see a food with **hydrogenated** or **partially hydrogenated** fat in it. It means an unsaturated oil has been made more saturated so it will be **solid at room temperature.** If you see hydrogenated on a label, think of it as a saturated fat.

Packed in water

Tuna or salmon packed in water instead of oil **has less fat.** Brands that are not low-salt can be put in a strainer and rinsed. This removes some of the salt—but not all of it.

Wheat flour

This refers to a white flour, not a whole wheat flour. **Whole wheat** or **whole grain** foods are better choices because they have more fiber.

Dairy foods

Nonfat or skim
Nonfat milk has ½g fat per cup or less.
This is the best choice for drinking.

Low-fat or 1%
This milk most often has 3g fat per cup.

Reduced-fat or 2%
This milk most often has 5g fat per cup.

Whole or homogenized
This milk almost always has 8g fat per cup.
For healthy diets, this is too much fat.

Half and half
Half and half has about 28g fat per cup.
This is a "forget you ever heard of it" type of food!

Heavy or whipping cream
A red flag should go up when you see this in any recipe. This has a whopping 88g fat per cup. Just picking this up can cause your arteries to harden! **Don't use** half and half or cream in recipes. Buttermilk or nonfat yogurt can often give like results and save you the fat.

Read all labels

Evaporated milk is just that

It's milk that has about 60% of the water taken out of it. (And you thought this came from evaporated cows.) Check the label before you buy. There is evaporated whole and evaporated nonfat (skim). The **best choice is evaporated nonfat.** Evaporated whole milk is best to avoid because 1 cup has 20g fat.

Powdered skim milk

This milk has no fat and is a healthy choice.

Buttermilk

Most buttermilk has no fat. (Regular buttermilk has 3g fat per cup.) This is the sour liquid that is left after churning butter from milk. It's a great choice because it's somewhat tart and rich like sour cream but **low in fat.** You might use this instead of milk in soups and sauces. Buttermilk may have too much salt for some people. Ask your doctor or registered dietitian about this.

Sour cream

This has 3g fat per tablespoon. Sour cream has a little over half of the fat of cream cheese, but it has about 12 times that of nonfat yogurt. That's a lot of fat. There is a reduced fat sour cream with about ⅓ less fat than regular, but that's still high.

   There is a no-fat sour cream, and this is a terrific product. You can make dressings or enrich soups with it. But be careful because sometimes it will separate when it's heated.

Read all labels

Ice cream, ice milk, frozen yogurt, sherbet, fruit sorbet

Ice creams contain a lot of fat. A premium ice cream (like Häagen Dazs) has as much as 17g of fat per 4 oz serving. But there are many other choices. (Ice milk has about 4g of fat per 4 oz serving and often doesn't cost that much.)

Frozen yogurt can be low-fat or nonfat. Nonfat is your best bet because it has **no** fat. Sherbet is made with milk or cream and has about the same amount of fat as ice milk. Fruit sorbets are really fruit ices and have no fat.

Almost all of these desserts contain sugar and are high in calories. There are many sugar-free choices on the market now, and you should look for them. A good example is **sugar-free nonfat frozen yogurt.**

Yogurt Dip

Yogurt

Buy nonfat yogurts. Low-fat yogurts still have 2 to 3g fat per 8 oz serving. Nonfat yogurt is a good choice for dressings, cold sauces and dips.

Cottage cheese (low-fat)

Low-fat cottage cheese has 2g of fat per serving. You can also buy no-fat cottage cheese. Cottage cheese has lots of salt in it, but there are some low-salt brands. Look for them.

Read all labels

Cream cheese

Most cream cheese has 11g fat per 1 oz serving. This stuff is too **high in fat** for any of us. Lower fat choices have about ⅓ less fat, but most still have 6 to 7g of fat per 1 oz serving. Fat-free cream cheese is good, but if used alone, you might not think it's so great. But try it on a bagel with a bit of All-Fruit and you are in fat-free heaven.

Cheese

Most cheese is **high in saturated fat,** but there are some good lower fat cheeses.

- Kraft 2% milk cheese is a good brand for both cheddar and Swiss. Each has about 5g of fat per oz.

- Farmer cheese and part skim mozzarella are good choices with about 4g of fat per oz.

- Some goat cheeses are low in fat with 4 to 5g per oz. These can be good for making an otherwise bland sauce rich and creamy.

Even some higher fat cheeses are OK—just **use them sparingly.** Parmesan has 10g of fat per oz, but ¼ oz of grated is about 2 tablespoons of cheese. This goes a long way in adding taste because aged cheeses like parmesan have a lot of flavor.

Almost all cheese has a lot of salt, so check out the Nutrition Facts on the label.

Fats

All fats have a lot of calories and should be eaten in small amounts. Here's what to do about these fats:

Butter
Butter has a lot of saturated fat and cholesterol. When you use it, **use it sparingly** like any other fat. There are times when using a soft margarine with no cholesterol and less fat is a better choice. Try the fat-free "I Can't Believe It's Not Butter" spray.

Margarine
The first ingredient should be a **liquid oil.** The **softer** the margarine the better. Buy a liquid or tub margarine. Buy one with twice as much unsaturated fat as saturated fat.

Mayonnaise
There are some great low-fat, low-cholesterol brands in the grocery store, or you can make your own.

Oils
Buy mono- or polyunsaturated oils. These include **canola, olive** and **peanut oil** (mono); and **safflower, sunflower, corn, cottonseed, sesame** and **soybean oil** (poly). **Stay away from** coconut, palm and palm kernel oil. These tropical oils have a lot of saturated fat.

Pure vegetable oil, 100% vegetable oil
Beware. This could be one of the saturated vegetable oils like coconut, palm or palm kernel oil.

Read all labels

Meats

Lean
This term is used when meat, poultry or seafood has no more than 10g of fat per 3 oz serving. Lean foods also have less than 4g of saturated fat and less than 95mg of cholesterol per serving.

Extra lean
This means no more than 5g of fat per 3 oz serving. Even better. If a food is extra lean, it must have less than 2g of saturated fat and less than 95mg of cholesterol per serving.

Read all labels

Other tricks to label reading

We have been talking about the terms on a label that first catch your eye. Here are some more tips for reading food labels.

Ingredients

Foods must have a list of what's in them on the label. Here's a sample from one popular cookie:

> ***Ingredients:*** *bleached flour, rolled oats, high fructose corn syrup, partially hydrogenated vegetable shortening (soybean and cottonseed oil), sugar, raisins, water, modified food starch, molasses, salt, baking soda, mono and diglycerides, cinnamon and artificial flavors.*

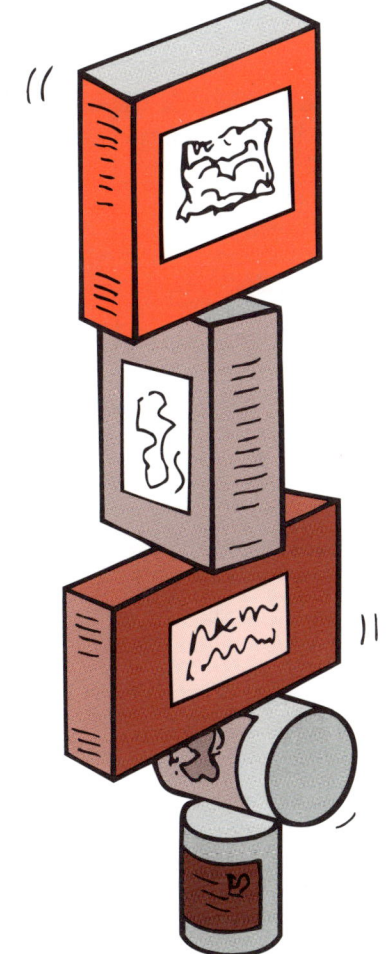

Ingredients are listed in the order of how much is in the food. The **first 3 ingredients** are the most important because they are in the greatest amount. If you see **sugar, corn syrup, honey, salt, oil** (any kind), **butter, lard** or **animal fat** as one of the first 3, steer clear. The food most likely has too much sugar, salt or fat for you.

If the ingredients say, "one or more of the following," watch out. You won't know which "one" is in the food. A label that says, "one or more of the following fats: coconut, safflower, cottonseed, palm or palm kernel oil," tells you very little.

Read all labels

Nutrition Facts label

You can check the Nutrition Facts and learn even more about a food. All foods must have these facts on their labels.* Look at the serving size and the nutrients per serving of this baked cheese ravioli dinner.

- First you find out how many **calories** are in each serving.

- The next part tells you how much **fat, cholesterol, sodium, carbohydrate** and **protein** is in the food.

- The label also tells what percent of your diet each of these adds up to. In this food, there is 18% of the sodium you can eat for the whole day. This isn't too much since this is a main dish.

- This food is also very low in fat and cholesterol—which is good for your diet.

The **percents** on a label are **based on a 2,000 calorie per day diet.** Check with a dietitian about how to figure the percents for your diet.

Nutrition Facts	
Serving Size 9.0 oz (240 grams)	
Servings Per Container 1	
Amount Per Serving	
Calories 250	Calories from Fat 18
	% Daily Value*
Total Fat 2g	3%
Saturated Fat Less than 1g	5%
Cholesterol 20mg	7%
Sodium 420mg	18%
Total Carbohydrate 44g	15%
Dietary Fiber 2g	8%
Sugars 4g	
Protein 14g	
Vitamin A 50% • Vitamin C 8%	
Calcium 25% • Iron 15%	

• Percent Daily Values are based on a 2,000 calorie diet. Your daily values may be higher or lower depending on your calorie needs:

		Calories	2,000	2,500
Total Fat	Less than		65g	80g
Sat Fat	Less than		20g	25g
Cholesterol	Less than		300mg	300mg
Sodium	Less than		2,400mg	2,400mg
Total Carbohydrate			300g	375g
Dietary Fiber			25g	30g

Calories per gram:
Fat 9 • Carbohydrates 4 • Protein 4

* *If the label is too small for a Nutrition Facts, there should be a toll free number you can call for this information.*

 Read all labels

Things you might not know about some foods

There are some foods that you might think are good choices for a healthy diet, but they really aren't. Here's how to choose what's best when you are shopping.

Avocados

Even though this is a fruit, it counts as fat—a big-time fat. Try not to eat much. One slice has about 4g of fat. The days of half an avocado with a dollop of mayo for lunch are gone!

Bacon

One slice of bacon has about 4g of fat—much of it saturated. This is too much fat for one teeny slice of bacon. You're better off to just avoid it.

Beef

Buy beef that is **lean** (less streaked with fat), and **trim off all excess fat.** Broil or grill meat on a rack. This way, fat drips through the rack while cooking, and you won't be eating it later.

Speaking of dripping fat—lean meats may seem higher priced, but that's not true if you count the fat that drips off in cooking. With a cheaper cut, you pay for fat that you don't get to eat.

The **hamburger** you find in the store can range anywhere from 7% fat by weight up to 30% fat. (You want hamburger that is **very red.** The more fat there is, the more pink the meat will be.)

If you don't see any ground beef in the 7 to 10% fat range, ask the butcher to grind you some. Tell him or her that a 10% (or less) fat content is what you need.

I'M GETTING A LITTLE TIRED OF ALL THIS CRITICISM...

Bread

Whole grain breads are the best bet for your body because they are higher in fiber. Make sure the label says **whole wheat** or **whole grain.**

Chicken

Buy breasts because these have the least fat. Take off the skin before you eat the chicken. **The skin has a lot of the fat.** If you are having dark meat, serve it with low-fat foods to keep the meal low in fat.

Chicken stock

There is nothing better than **fresh** chicken stock, but it takes a lot of time to make. If you use "store-bought," be careful. Most canned chicken stock has lots of salt, but there are some low-salt versions, too. Look for those. Herb-Ox and Featherweight make a salt-free bouillon in powder form, and they are pretty good. Some low-salt bouillon has a lot of potassium and magnesium in it, so ask your doctor if this bouillon is OK for you.

Eggs

The American Heart Association says that 3 eggs a week is OK even on a restricted diet.

The problem with eggs is in the yolks. That's where all the cholesterol is. An egg yolk also has about 5g of fat. To cut back on the fat and cholesterol, use one whole egg with two egg whites for an omelet. Using egg substitutes is good because most are low in both cholesterol and fat.

Things you might not know

Fish

You most likely have heard that **fish is low in fat and cholesterol.** Well, it is, and here's what to do about fish:

- ✓ When you can, buy fresh or flash-frozen fish.

- ✓ Fillets are the easiest to cook and eat.

- ✓ Some shellfish, like shrimp, is high in cholesterol. But because it has less fat, you can eat it now and then.

- ✓ **Grill, broil, bake, poach or steam** fish. The flavor really comes out that way (less fat, too).

Fruits

High in fiber; low in fat, cholesterol and salt. Healthy choices are fresh, canned (not syrup), frozen (without sugar) or dried.

Ham

A big ol' cured ham is high in fat and salt. The sliced ham you can find in the lunch meat case has less fat. Most of the fat in sliced ham has been trimmed off. Look for those labeled 98%, 99% or 100% fat-free by weight. Sliced ham is still high in salt but not so much that you can't eat it once in a while. (It may not be OK for those on very low-salt diets. Ask your doctor.)

Nuts

Nuts are very high in fat. An ounce of nuts has as much fat as a tablespoon of oil. Eat nuts alone or use them in a recipe only now and then. Don't eat the nuts that have a high saturated fat content. These include: **macadamias, brazils** and **cashews.**

Organ meats

Foods like liver, sweetbreads, kidneys, brains, tripe and chitterlings are high in cholesterol. (If iron is needed in your diet, 3 to 4 oz of liver once a week is OK. But don't cook liver with a saturated fat. Cholesterol in liver plus saturated fat is not a good combination.)

Pasta

This stuff is good for you. It is high in complex carbohydrates. Colored pastas like spinach, tomato or whole wheat have nice flavors. They make it easier to cook a tasty dish without having to add a lot of other things that are high in fat and salt (like cheeses and cream sauces).

Pork

The tenderloin is the best cut of pork to use. Buy small tenderloins. They seem to be more tender. **Trim them of all fat** before cooking.

Things you might not know

Pig's feet

Pig's feet are too high in fat to eat often. Most of the time they are pickled which means they have a lot of salt. Eat these only once in a while if you just can't live without them.

Rice

Brown rice is better for you than white rice because it has more fiber. White rice has had the outer hull stripped off, leaving you with soft goo when you cook it. (**Enriched** white rice does have many nutrients.) Try the brown and white side-by-side. You will find that the brown rice has a nice nutty flavor.

Roast

Rib roast is too high in fat to use. Pot roast with gravy is not a good idea either. Fat from the roast ends up in the gravy. If you like roast, use a rump, shoulder or eye of the round roast. **Trim off all excess fat.** Roast it on a rack to let the fat drip off.

Shellfish

Scallops, clams, oysters and **mussels** are low in fat and have almost no cholesterol. Buy them fresh because the canned ones have lots of salt. Because of pollution, there is risk in eating these raw. It's a good idea to cook these guys.

Shrimp, lobsters and **crabs** are types of shellfish known as crustaceans. These types of seafood have **lots of cholesterol** but very little fat. If you cook them in water, and not butter or other fat, they are OK to eat now and then.

Shrimp is sold by size or "count." This system measures the shrimp by the number per pound. For example, "16-20" would mean that there are 16 to 20 raw pieces of shrimp in a pound. This is a good size to buy because the shrimp will be about 1 oz each. If your diet calls for 2 oz of meat at a meal, you can eat 2 of these larger shrimp.

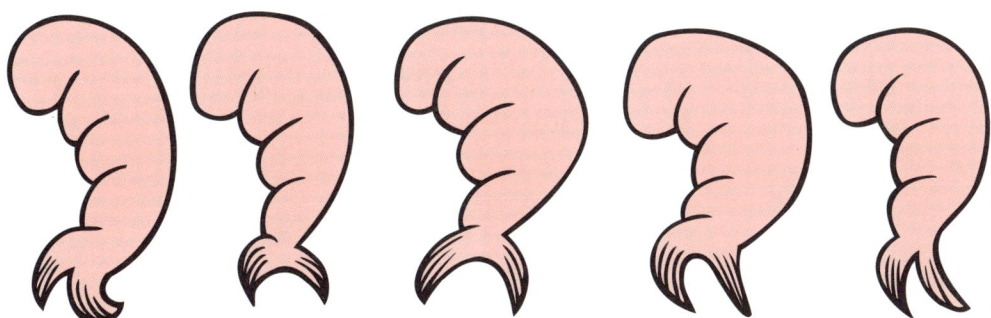

Steak

Buy beef that is **lean** (less streaked with fat), and **trim off all excess fat.** Some of the leaner cuts are london broil, top sirloin or flank steak.

Things you might not know

Sugar

It's not a good idea to eat too much sugar because it is loaded with calories. **Saccharin** is OK in very small amounts, but large amounts might be a cancer risk. Many companies sweeten foods with **aspartame.** You can buy both products in packets or tablets. Both saccharin and aspartame break down in cooking and lose the sweet flavor.

Tongue

Beef tongue is high in fat and cholesterol and is not a good choice. (1 oz has 6g of fat.)

Turkey

The part of the turkey with the least fat is the breast. You can buy turkey breasts by themselves as well as sliced breast fillets. These are great foods. If you're going to roast a whole turkey, **do not buy a "self-basting" model.** They are self-basting because margarine or some other fat has been injected under the breasts.

Vegetables

Fresh vegetables, frozen vegetables (without salt or sauce) and low-salt or no salt added vegetables are best for you. When cooking fresh vegetables, just steam and eat them. They taste best in the nude!

Things you might not know

Food for thought

✓ Eat more fruits and vegetables.

✓ Eat more low-fat meats like chicken, turkey, fish or lean cuts of pork or beef.

✓ Eat less high-fat meats like untrimmed or fatty cuts of beef and pork, lamb, organ meats, bacon and sausage.

✓ Eat less high-fat cheeses.

✓ Eat skim milk dairy foods.

✓ Eat more whole grain breads and cereals, pasta, corn and dried beans or peas.

Things you might not know

Eating out

Most of us eat out or order "take-out" at least once a week—maybe more. Before you order take-out or go to a restaurant, get your mind set: **You can special order ANYTHING.** Here's what to do.

✗ Stay away from:
- fried chicken, fried fish sandwiches
- burgers with cheese and lots of mayo
- shakes, french fries
- chips and dip, nachos, potato skins
- cheese enchiladas, refried beans, guacamole
- deluxe pizzas (with meats, extra cheese, anchovies, etc.)
- gyros
- cream soups, french onion soup
- spinach salads with bacon dressing
- "loaded" baked potatoes (with cheese, bacon, etc.)
- pasta salads with lots of mayo or with heavy oil and vinegar dressings

✗ Stay away from fried or breaded foods. These foods are high in fat and salt.

✓ Order **baked, broiled, steamed, poached** or **grilled** foods without breading, butter or sauces. Also ask that no fat or seasonings be added.

✓ Order **salad dressings or sauces on the side.** That way you can limit the amount you put on. A good rule of thumb is to use no more than **2 teaspoons** of a sauce or dressing.

✓ Some breads will have butter or salt on them. Ask for **plain bread or rolls.** Croissants, cracklin' corn bread, muffins, Danish or sweet rolls are not good choices. They are high in fat and salt.

✓ If you order a baked potato, using a tablespoon of sour cream is better than a tablespoon of butter or margarine. Or try just fresh pepper on the potato. It really spices up the flavor.

✓ If a salad has bacon, egg or cheddar cheese on it, ask for a plain salad, or see what **other toppings** they offer.

✓ Use **milk in your coffee or tea** rather than coffee creamer or half and half. Ask your server to bring you some.

✓ Servings in restaurants are often large. Split a main course with someone at your table, or take home a **doggie bag.**

✓ Many meats have fat on them. As you would at home, **trim off the fat,** and leave it on your plate.

✓ If you have a cocktail, have a white wine spritzer or a light beer to save calories.

✓ Save high-fat or very rich desserts for special times only. The fat can really add up here. If the dessert is rich, have only **a few bites.** Split it with others at the table. Your best bet is to **order fresh fruits for dessert.**

✓ Decide where you are going **before** you leave home. Ask yourself, "Do they have foods that I want to eat?"

✓ If you are trying a new restaurant, **call ahead.** Ask the manager if they can fix low-fat, low-cholesterol or low-salt foods.

These menu words can clue you in on which foods might be best for you.

✓ **OK:** *steamed, fresh, grilled, broiled, fat-free, oil-free, roasted.* Low-calorie may also be OK, but check it out. It may have lots of salt or not be truly low-calorie.

✗ **Not OK:** *butter sauce, buttery, sautéed, fried, au gratin, hollandaise, bernaise, basted, scalloped, crisp.* Don't eat foods fixed this way. Au jus served on the side may be OK if it's thin and not thick and fatty or salty.

Here are some clues that may help you decide which foods to eat in ethnic restaurants.

- **Asian foods** often have a lot of MSG (monosodium glutamate) — a type of salt. They also fry many foods like egg rolls, won tons and dumplings. Order steamed foods or lean meat and vegetables stir fried in very little oil. Tell them to hold the MSG.

- **Greek foods** may have a lot of feta cheese, lamb and beef (high-fat). Broiled or baked dishes, salads without feta cheese, and pita bread are good choices here.

- **Indian foods** often have sauces; many are made with yogurt. Ask what is in them and how they are fixed. Tandori dishes are good choices, as are many vegetable dishes. Ask them to **go easy on the oil** in making your dishes.

- **Italian foods** are often made with oils, sauces and butter (high-fat). Choose tomato-based sauces like marinara.

- **Mexican foods** may have a lot of beef and cheese (high-fat). Stay away from chips and dip, nachos, refried beans, sour cream and guacamole. Tacos and burritos made with chicken are better choices. One dollop of guacamole on your dish would be OK. Ask if they have fat-free or low-fat sour cream. If not, and you really like sour cream with Mexican foods, next time you eat there take some with you.

Eating out 39

Cooking it yourself

Changing the **way** you cook can help you cut down on fat, cholesterol and salt. For example:

NOT SO GOOD	A BETTER CHOICE
fried	poached, broiled, grilled
basted	steamed
braised	stir fried (with little oil)
stewed	roasted
breaded	baked (without breading)

There are lots of places to look to learn new ways of cooking. Here is a list of just a few of the good cookbooks and magazines you can find:

**American Heart Association
Low-Fat, Low-Cholesterol Cookbook**
Scott Grundy, MD, PhD, Editor
Times Books

The Eating Well Rush Hour Cookbook
Eating Well Books

Eat Smart for a Healthy Heart
Carolyn E. Moore, PhD, RD and
Denton A. Cooley, MD
Barron's Educational Publishers

Graham Kerr's Creative Choices Cookbook
Perigree Publishing

The Living Heart Cookbook
Antonio M. Grotto Jr., MD, DPhil
Fireside Publishing

The Moosewood Cookbook
Mollie Katzen
Ten Speed Press

Cooking Light Magazine
Southern Living Publications

Eating Well Magazine
EW Communications, LP

Any one of these has great suggestions on meal planning, snacks, desserts and plain or fancy dinners. You can find recipes for almost any food you ever wanted to eat (and even a few foods that you don't).

MEASURING UP

It's good to know the different measures and how they compare with each other.

LIQUIDS

3 teaspoons = 1 tablespoon

2 tablespoons = 1 fluid ounce

1 cup = 8 ounces

16 tablespoons = 1 cup

2 cups = 1 pint

2 pints = 1 quart

4 quarts = 1 gallon

DRY

1 weight ounce = 28 grams

16 ounces = 1 pound

453 grams = 1 pound

1 gram = 1000 milligrams

1 teaspoon of dry ingredients = about 4 grams

Cooking tips

You may want to change some of your favorite recipes to meet your new way of eating. Here's how to do that.

- **Compare a recipe in a heart cookbook** with a recipe for a dish that you often make. List the ingredients in your "old" recipe that you think might be replaced with more healthy choices. Here are some things that work just as well:

OLD RECIPE	A BETTER CHOICE
sour cream	low- or no-fat sour cream
real eggs	egg substitute
ground beef	ground turkey breast or lean ground beef
butter	vegetable oil
cheddar cheese	farmer cheese

- If a recipe calls for oil, **use a mono- or poly-unsaturated oil.** (See the list of these on page 7.) Sometimes you can even leave out the oil. Applesauce can be used instead of oil in some baked foods like brownies, cakes and even corn bread.

- When you have to cook in a pan, use a spray oil like Pam. Pam also makes a spray olive oil. (Use only a little of any oil.)

Cooking it yourself

To cut salt when cooking:

- Season with herb powders, leaves or seeds, not salts. In the spice section of your grocery, you will find onion salt, garlic salt, celery salt and seasoned salt. Don't buy these. Anything in the spice rack called a "salt" is one.

- Don't use these foods if you are eating less salt:

  ✗ teriyaki sauce   ✗ barbecue sauce
  ✗ soy sauce   ✗ sardines
  ✗ tamari sauce   ✗ anchovies
  ✗ worcestershire sauce   ✗ olives, pimentos

  Ask your doctor or dietitian if the foods below can be on your diet. If they can, do this: Rinse these foods with water before you eat them. Rinsing will remove some of the salt but not all of it. Eat very little of these foods.

  ✗ canned salmon, tuna   ✗ canned clams, oysters

- A lot of people use lemon juice instead of salt. This works pretty well for some dishes even though lemon juice tastes nothing like salt. Start with a little bit and build up.

- You can find many herb mixtures in the grocery. These give you good flavor without salt. Some brands are: McCormick, Mrs. Dash and Spice Islands.

Cooking it yourself 43

Some tips to cut fat when cooking:

- **Eat vegetables "clean"** (with no sauce, butter or breading). Steam your vegetables, and learn to season them with herbs and spices (pages 45-46).

    Vegetables with sauces aren't bad for you if you cut down on the fat that goes into the sauces. Vegetable casseroles and other vegetarian dishes can be tasty and healthy. When the meat and other fats are left out of the meal, more can be done to the vegetables.

- **Drain or rinse off all excess fat** when cooking. This is easy to do when cooking ground beef. Use a strainer, and press down on the cooked meat with a large spoon. This will squeeze out the extra fat. Before you put the meat back in the pan, wipe all the grease out of the pan with a paper towel.

- When making soups and stews, cool them in the fridge until solid fat forms on top. **Skim off the fat** and throw it away.

Cooking with herbs & spices

Herbs are the leaves of certain plants. Spices are the seeds.

Play around with new herbs and spices to find out what tastes good to you. Over time your tastes will change, and you won't miss the salt. Here's how to get started:

- Each month buy a jar of herbs or spices that you've never tried before. Try fresh herbs, too, when you can find them (or grow some).

- Dried herbs and spices are stronger than fresh ones. **Don't use too much of a dried herb or spice the first time.** A rule of thumb: If you can stand the same amount of ground black pepper, you will probably like that much of a dried herb or spice. If you use too much at first, it may turn you off to the taste.

- If you use **fresh herbs,** use about 3 times more than you would of a dried herb.

- Try an herb or spice by itself when you first use it. This gives you a good idea of the flavor. If you don't like it, toss it out and buy another. You won't like all herbs and spices.

Cooking it yourself 45

- A good place to start is with this recipe. It's simple, and the flavor of any herb or spice will come through.

LAZY CHICKEN BREASTS (2 servings)

2 ....3 oz chicken breasts
(on bone, skinned and trimmed of fat)

2 tsp ....olive oil or "I Can't Believe It's Not Butter" spray

¼ tsp........dried rosemary
(or any single herb/spice)

- Place the chicken breasts in a baking pan.
- Put 1 tsp of olive oil or spray on top of each breast.
- Sprinkle the herb of your choice over each breast.
- Let them take a nap (uncovered) in a preheated 350° oven for about 25 minutes.
- Wake them now and then to make sure they are not getting too much sleep.

Some other good herbs and spices to try with this chicken are:

basil
oregano
thyme
tarragon
caraway seeds
curry powder
marjoram
garlic or onion powder

- Once you know what you like, you're ready to combine some herbs and spices. Look for recipes that have more than one herb, and try them first.

More food talk

The main idea of this book is to learn how to eat less fat, cholesterol and salt. Besides this, there are other facts about food that your doctor or dietitian may want you to know.

More food talk

Food groups

When you were a kid, you might have learned that healthy eating was to eat from 4 food groups: meats, dairy foods, fruits and vegetables, and breads. Most likely no one told you much more than this. As you grew older, your food groups may have become sweets, fat, salt and alcohol. The result of this for many of us was ending up in our doctor's office with him or her saying, "Change your diet or else."

No one food group can give your body all that it needs. You need a **balance** of many foods. This is why you will hear, "Eat a variety of foods each day." The food pyramid (on the next page) can help you do this. It shows you the kinds and number of servings of foods that make up a healthy diet.

The foods at the base of the pyramid are the building blocks of a good diet. These are what you should eat more of. As you follow the pyramid up, amounts to eat decrease. Oils and fats are at the top. This means you should eat the least number of servings of these.

Fiber

Fiber is the part of food that your body doesn't digest. Some foods that have lots of fiber in them are:
- fruits
- vegetables
- whole grains
- cereals

There is a lot of talk that fiber may lower cholesterol and reduce the risk of some kinds of cancer. So far, studies have not proved either of these.

We do know that fiber is good for your digestion and can keep you from having problems like constipation and diverticulosis.

Eating more fiber will most likely mean you will be eating foods that are good for you. Most of the foods high in fiber are also low in fat, cholesterol and salt. There are exceptions to this (like some store-bought bran muffins), so you have to read the labels carefully.

Fiber also gives you a feeling of fullness. This can help with hunger as you decrease the amount of fat and/or calories in your diet.

More food talk

More about cholesterol

Cholesterol doesn't just float around in the blood by itself. It is carried around in the blood by **lipoproteins.** There are 2 main types: **HDL** (high density lipoproteins) and **LDL** (low density lipoproteins).

Lipoproteins work sort of like a bus system. Some of the buses carry cholesterol to the cells, and others carry it away from the cells. LDL-buses carry cholesterol to the cells. If you have too much LDL, you end up with a traffic jam. Blood vessels may get clogged.

Cholesterol is picked up by HDL and taken to the liver where the body can get rid of it. **HDL helps to unclog the system.** With more HDL, there is less cholesterol in the blood to team up with fat and clog your arteries.

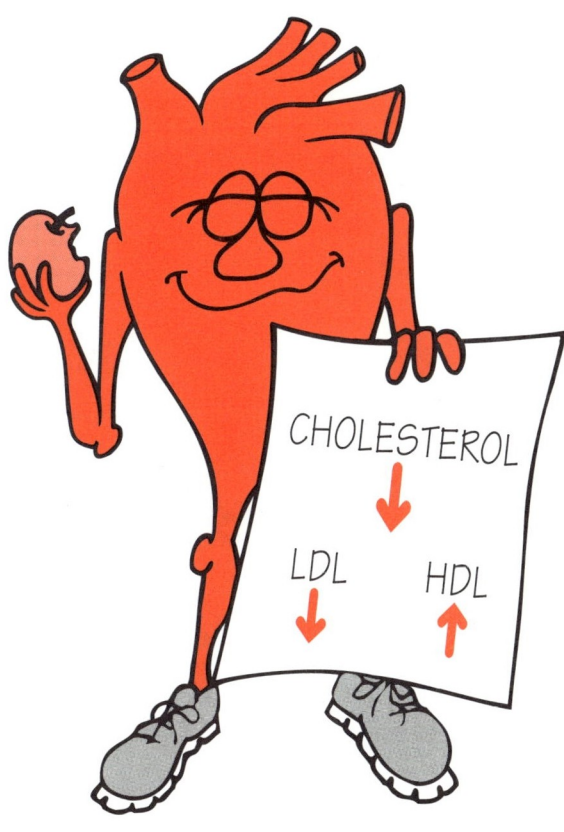

Your doctor may ask you to aim for a total blood cholesterol of 180 or less, with an HDL level between 40 and 70 and an LDL of less than 100.

You may lower your LDL or raise your HDL by:
- *eating low-fat, low-cholesterol foods*
- *regular exercise*
- *not smoking*
- *eating unsaturated fats when fats are part of your diet*

Protein

You may think of protein as just meat. Well, there is a lot of protein in meat, but protein is in a lot of other foods such as:

- milk
- spaghetti noodles
- low-fat and fat-free cheese
- yogurt
- cottage cheese
- lima beans, kidney beans, black-eyed peas
- egg substitutes
- oatmeal
- brown rice
- Special K cereal

Not all of these foods have the same amount of protein.

A lot of protein comes from plants. Most of us eat about 3 times as much animal protein as we do plant protein. It's a good idea to try and get that closer to about the same amount of each.

You can go further and eat an all vegetable diet. Being a vegetarian can be good for you, but you have to be careful. Some vegetables don't have complete proteins. To be complete, a protein has to have all of the amino acids (the building blocks of proteins). For example, rice doesn't have complete proteins, and some beans don't have complete proteins. But if you eat rice and beans together, you get all the amino acids your body needs. (Good news if you like red beans and rice!)

There's a good book called *Diet for a Small Planet*. (Most bookstores carry it.) It can help you plan a vegetarian diet. A registered dietitian can help, too.

Last thing. Believe it or not, you don't have to eat a lot of meat to keep your muscles strong. You can get some of the protein you need from other sources. You can be a lean, mean, fightin' machine by eating a diet with less meat.

Carbohydrates

Carbohydrates are sugars, and there are 2 kinds: **complex** and **simple.**

Complex carbohydrates are found in starches and vegetables like:

- bread
- pasta
- corn
- beans and peas
- potatoes

Simple carbohydrates are things like table sugar (sucrose) and fruit sugar (fructose). More refined sugars, like table sugar, are in cakes, ice cream and candies. These foods often have a lot of saturated fat in them, too.

Fruits are a simple carbohydrate, but they are high in fiber and vitamins and good for you. If you like sweets, fresh, canned or dried fruits are a good choice.

More food talk

Calories

Eating a lean, lower-fat diet in moderate amounts and exercising regularly will lead to weight loss most of the time.

But a word of warning: Just because a food says low-fat or no-fat doesn't mean it doesn't have calories. **Some low-fat foods have a lot of calories.** This is because food companies will put in sugars or proteins to make up for the reduced fat. Sometimes the food is not lower in calories.

Look at the Nutrition Facts on the label. Check not only the fat grams, but the number of calories and the amount of protein and carbohydrate.

More food talk

Bye!

This is not the end for you, but a starting place. What you have learned here is a base for healthy eating. There are other places to learn more, and some of them are mentioned in this book.

Again, here are the high points. Eat:

- lean meats, poultry or fish
  (or low-fat protein choices)
- skim milk (or nonfat) dairy products
- fruits and vegetables
- less salt
- more complex carbohydrates

There are new, healthier foods coming on the market all the time. Read all food labels. Make sure that foods really are what the producer claims.

It takes awhile to feel good about your new way of eating, but in time, it becomes second nature. Here's to your health!